Daily Encouragement

for Homeschooling Mothers

Charlene Notgrass

Daily Encouragement for Homeschooling Mothers
Charlene Notgrass

Copyright © 2004, 2013 Notgrass Company

ISBN 978-1-60999-054-1

Notgrass Company
975 Roaring River Road
Gainesboro, Tennessee 38562
1-800-211-8793
www.notgrass.com

Get more daily encouragement at Charlene's blog:
notgrass.com/daily

For homeschool curriculum written by Charlene and her family:
notgrass.com

For Molly Perry,
a sensible, pure, kind,
young woman,
who works at home,
who loves and is subject
to her husband,
and who loves her children.

Precious Homeschooling Mother,

I admire homeschooling mothers. You love your children deeply and make daily sacrifices to do what you believe is best for them. You are one of my heroines. I know that there are days when you don't feel like a heroine at all. On those days you need encouragement.

The heart of this book comes from Titus 2:3-5, where Paul gives instructions about godly characteristics and behavior for older women and for younger women. Though these verses give wisdom for all women, there are specific lessons here for the homeschooling mother.

Paul speaks first about older women. He begins by listing two behaviors they must avoid: malicious gossip and enslavement to much wine. Next, he gives older women a trait that they must make part of their lives: they must be reverent in their behavior. Finally, Paul tells older women something they must do: they must teach what is good.

Paul states the reason why older women should do this. He wants them to help young women by encouraging them to:

Love their husbands.
Love their children.
Be sensible.
Be pure.
Be workers at home.
Be kind.
Be subject to their own husbands.

As I write this to you, I speak as an older woman. If you were to look at my driver's license, you would know for certain that I fall into that category. I'd like to think that you couldn't tell by looking at me, but my guess is that it is as obvious as the driver's license. A popular phrase in the 1960s was "Don't trust anyone over thirty!" I was born in 1953, so I passed that thirty mark years ago. Should you trust me? I am not writing to you as an expert. I'm just a fallible woman who has lived and loved, gained and lost, failed and succeeded, sinned and been forgiven. I am not at all like Mary Poppins—practically perfect in every way. I am more like Jo in *Little Women*—hopelessly flawed.

The women that Paul encouraged Titus to teach were also hopelessly flawed—the older ones and the younger ones. I'm sure that you go to bed each night knowing it is true for you, too. If older women and younger women are all fallible, why does Paul give older women responsibility for teaching younger ones? Perhaps one reason is that we have had so many experiences living, loving, gaining, losing, failing, succeeding, sinning and being forgiven.

Since I married my husband Ray in 1974, I have been amazed at his knowledge. I call Ray my dictionary, encyclopedia, and Bible concordance. Sometimes when I am once again dumbfounded at his knowledge, I'll ask, "How did you know that?" and he tells me again, "I pay attention."

I think one advantage of being older is that we have had longer to pay attention. All that living, loving, gaining, and losing teaches us, if we pay attention. In Psalm 37:25, the psalmist writes: "I have been young and now I am old, yet I have not seen the righteous forsaken or his descendants begging bread." He had been paying attention.

One advantage of age is learning that there is gain after loss, joy after sorrow, relief after pain. We have simply lived long enough to experience that over and over again. We have learned that God is with us in all of life, when things are going the way we want them to and when they are not.

Older women also know that problems have solutions. We learn that problems do not mean that God doesn't love us anymore; they really mean that He does.

In Job we learn that God does not cause our suffering. However, He does allow it. I believe that this allowing is a form of His discipline. "For those whom the Lord loves He disciplines . . . ." (Hebrews 12:6). "For to you it has been granted for Christ's sake, not only to believe in Him, but also to suffer for His sake" (Philippians 1:29).

One of the most positive women I have known was my friend Irene. How I admire this Christian lady who lived to be ninety-seven. I knew her for her last twenty-seven years. She was a widow for twenty-five of them. When Irene was a young woman, health issues made her infertile after giving birth to one daughter. She lost a breast to cancer around age forty.

"All discipline for the moment seems not to be joyful, but sorrowful; yet to those who have been trained by it, afterwards it yields the peaceful fruit of righteousness" (Hebrews 12:11). Irene's life had the peaceful fruit of righteousness. Her righteousness showed in many ways: in attitude, in service, and in generosity. When our children were young, she would invite them over to play croquet and board games. Irene regularly transported a blind lady in her nineties to church. One Sunday Irene fell on the ice and broke her cheekbone while doing that. When volunteers remodeled our church building, there was Irene with a brush staining molding.

Of course, it is not age alone that teaches us. The wise older woman has learned from God's word and from walking in the footsteps of Jesus for many years.

My life has been richer because I have learned from Irene and many other older women. The first was my mother. So many of her words from my childhood are impressed on my heart, and I am blessed to continue hearing them every day. Another was my Sunday School teacher, Miss Dovie, who continued to encourage me even after I had grown children of my own. I admired her gentleness and her spunk. She mounted a horse on her hundredth birthday. When I was a young mother, I learned from several older women in our congregation. Many of the choices I have made in my mothering, I learned from the words and lives of those women.

I hope your life is blessed by godly older women. If it is not, please try to find at least one that you can bless. You will be blessed in return.

In these pages, I have shared God's Word and I have shared my heart. Through photographs I have also shared my little corner of the world.

I'd like to tell you about my little corner. After years of praying and searching for a piece of the countryside that would fit our very small budget, we found a beautiful spot with a very old, drafty house and an unbelievably low price tag. We have been enjoying the beauty, fixing up the house, and trying to figure out how to stay warm in the winter since 2003. Let me give you an idea of just how much fixing there was to do. A few months after we moved in, I visited our small town museum and met two ladies from the county historical society. When I introduced myself, I said that we had bought the Crabtree house on the Gore farm. One of them hugged me and said, "We were afraid someone would tear it down."

I took each photograph in *Daily Encouragement* in our yard or a short walk from our home. We are blessed to live in a beautiful area. I like what our daughter-in-law Audra said when she visited here for the first time: "It's like living in a calendar." I agree. I thank God for bringing us here.

I marvel at the world God created—the big things like mountains and the little things like leaves on a wall. Many of the photos I have chosen simply show God's creations in their natural settings. Some are of Roaring River, which rarely roars these days. Others are of our neighbor's pretty barn and pasture. I have included several of the stone walls and iron fence of the cemetery just beyond our backyard. People buried in the oldest graves there were living, loving, gaining, losing, failing, succeeding, sinning and being forgiven before the Civil War.

I also included photos of my flower garden. God has made the climate so perfect and the ground so rich here in this river bottom that even I can have a flower garden. I used to feel sorry for any plant that came into my home, because I knew it was not going to be in the world much longer. I would surely kill it or ignore it until it faded away. However, I was determined that here I would have a flower garden.

Flower gardens grow like children do, little by little and day by day. Our job is to be patient while they do. We must be attentive gardeners: tending, nurturing, training, and loving like only a mother can do.

Paul didn't just talk about mothering in Titus 2, he talked about being wives as well. I encourage you to take care of your marriage. My heart aches for the young adults I know personally who are suffering because of their parents' divorces after they grew up. Some are homeschool graduates. While you are tending your garden, your home, and your children, tend to your marriage, too.

The format of *Daily Encouragement* is simple. Each page is for one day and has one principle that can be implemented that very day. I've included thirty-one principles, one for each day of the month. Just take a few minutes each day to read and reflect— and then put Titus 2 into practice.

Keep *Daily Encouragement* where you can find it easily. If you're like me, don't put it on your desk—you might never see it again! You can't ever be behind because you simply read page 4 on the 4th of the month and page 15 on the 15th of the month, etc. If you miss a day, a week, or even a year, you can always find your place (if you can find your book!). If you are very organized and actually read it all in a month, just start over again the next month.

Welcome to my heart and my corner. I hope you find your daily visits refreshing. May God bless you and your home.

Charlene Notgrass

Loving Your Husband: In Your Thoughts

Your husband knows that he falls short of being the man he wants to be. You've noticed that too, but today he is not going to hear about that from you. Your husband also does things that are true, honorable, right, pure, lovely, of good repute, excellent, and worthy of praise. Today think about those things. Choose five things you appreciate about your husband and tell him what they are.

Finally, brethren, whatever is true, whatever is honorable,
whatever is right, whatever is pure, whatever is lovely,
whatever is of good repute, if there is any excellence
and if anything worthy of praise, dwell on these things.
Philippians 4:8

Loving Your Children: Be Their Mother

You are a homeschooling mother. It's easy to get bogged down in that first word "homeschooling," and not concentrate enough on the second one, being a mother. Children need a mother—a sweet, soft, cushy, loving, kind, gentle, devoted, caring mother. Concentrate today on the mother part. Give extra hugs, kisses, and cuddles. Think of something especially mothering you can do. Perhaps you could sing a lullaby or hold your child in your lap and read a bedtime story. Your son might be sixteen years old and might not have heard a lullaby in years, but try it just for fun.

But we proved to be gentle among you,
as a nursing mother tenderly cares
for her own children.
1 Thessalonians 2:7

Loving Your Children: Trust God's Choice

Be confident. Out of all the women in the world—out of all the women in the history of the world—God chose you to be the mother of your children. That's right. You. Fallible you. Worried you. Sinful you. Trust His choice. No one on earth can be a better mother for your children than you can. Don't be afraid that you cannot give them what they need. Thank God today for making you the mother of your children.

Behold, children are a gift of the Lord,
The fruit of the womb is a reward.
Psalm 127:3

Being Sensible: Pray

At many times during your homeschool journey, you have wondered if you are covering everything. Now be sensible. The universe is everything. You are not going to cover it, so get over it! Only God can give your children everything they need. Today pray instead of worrying about it.

*Be anxious for nothing, but in everything by
prayer and supplication with thanksgiving
let your requests be made known to God.
And the peace of God,
which surpasses all comprehension,
will guard your hearts
and your minds in Christ Jesus.
Philippians 4:6–7*

Being Pure: Be Sure to Shelter

Do people ever accuse you of sheltering your children? Instead of being defensive, be thankful for the wonderful opportunity to shelter. Do you sometimes make the mistake of allowing your children to see, hear, or read something impure? Don't you feel terrible after that? Did you learn the Sunday School song that teaches us, "Be careful, little eyes, what you see"? It's true. Our Father up above is looking down in love, so we must be careful what we allow our children to experience. It isn't true that it doesn't matter what a child reads as long as he is reading something. Purity matters. Today make sure that your children experience only what is pure. It's worth it, even if your child misses out on something popular.

Blessed are the pure in heart,
For they shall see God.
Matthew 5:8

Being a Worker at Home: Be a Home Maker

We have emphasized the mother part of being a "homeschooling mother." Now let's emphasize the home part. All of us are homemakers. Help your children think of home as a place of simple beauty. Are you a gifted homemaker? Give yourself permission to start, continue, or finish a fun project today. Is homemaking a challenge for you? Try something simple. Put a vase or bottle of wildflowers in the bathroom, set a basket of fruit in the center of a table, put construction paper or gift wrapping paper behind your children's artwork and make a pretty art display. Just remember your favorite landscape, and you will be reminded of how God feels about beauty.

Out of the ground the Lord God caused to
grow every tree that is pleasing to the sight . . . .
Genesis 2:9

Being Kind:
Teach Your Children to Be Kind

At night when we lie awake thinking about how we are doing with our children, we may wonder when our child will learn to read . . . or multiply . . . or understand the periodic table. Sometimes upcoming achievement tests increase our anxieties, as we worry about how our children will do on the tests. One day our children will be among all the nations gathered around Jesus. He is going to talk to them and to us about feeding the hungry, giving drink to the thirsty, inviting in strangers, clothing the naked, and going to the sick and to those in prison—not about reading, math, and science. Today give your children an opportunity to be kind.

Little children, let us not love with word or with tongue, but in deed and truth.
1 John 3:18

Being Subject to Your Husband: Give Him His Preference

Your husband has preferences. Show your submission today by giving him at least one of his preferences. Wear his favorite color. Put his favorite sheets on the bed. Leave the green peppers out of the meatloaf this time, if he doesn't like them. I don't know what your husband's preferences are, but you do. Do something today to show him that what he wants is important to you.

*Do nothing from selfishness
or empty conceit,
but with humility of mind
regard one another
as more important than yourselves;
do not merely look out
for your own personal interests,
but also for the interests of others.
Philippians 2:3–4*

Loving Your Husband: Give Him You

With your days filled with homeschooling responsibilities, it is sometimes easy to give your husband the dregs—you know, what is left over after you've given to everyone else all day. Don't do that today. Give your husband yourself. If you were giving a special present to someone, you might buy pretty wrapping paper and put a fancy bow on top. Wrap yourself up in your prettiest clothes and give your husband a big smile when he comes home from working for you and your children. Look so good that your children will ask you if you're going somewhere.

He who finds a wife finds a good thing
and obtains favor from the Lord.
Proverbs 18:22

Loving Your Children: Teach Them

You have important lessons to impart to your children. Solomon told his son:

Hear, my son, your father's instruction and do not forsake your mother's teaching; Indeed, they are a graceful wreath to your head and ornaments about your neck.
Proverbs 1:8-9

Your children need the teaching of their mother. Be confident that you personally have lessons to teach them. What is something you want to make sure they learn above all else? Impart a life lesson.

Loving Your Children: Discipline Them

Benjamin Franklin is credited with this statement: "Let the child's first lesson be obedience, and the second will be what thou wilt." Today make sure that your children obey you, not just in certain areas but in everything. Now that takes hard work. You have to be diligent. It's hard to follow through and make sure your child obeys your every command. Which of God's commands do you want your child to omit? Letting him ignore your instructions teaches him that he can ignore God's commands, too.

A wise son makes a father glad,
But a foolish son is a grief to his mother.
Proverbs 10:1

Being Sensible: Use Life's Interruptions, Too

God told Moses one important way He wanted Israelite children to learn about Himself: He wanted Israelite parents to train their children as they went about their daily lives. Sometimes we see life's interruptions as enemies to our homeschooling. Today be thankful for each interruption. Maybe God is trying to get your attention. Tell your children why you choose to respond to your interruptions the way you do. When Jesus came, He trained His disciples by allowing them to be with Him. Think about how He responded to the interruptions He faced. Remember the woman who interrupted Him on His way to raise Jairus' daughter (Mark 5).

And He appointed twelve, so that
they would be with Him and that
He could send them out to preach.
Mark 3:14

Being Pure: Center Your Homeschooling in God's Word

Center your homeschooling in the Word of God. No other subject measures up to its importance. Today share the pure milk of the Word with your children. Help your children know Jesus, the Word who became flesh (John 1:14). Help them act upon what they have learned so they can be like a wise man (Matthew 7:24-27). Prepare their hearts to be honest and good so they will hear the word and bear fruit (Luke 8:11-15). Help them know the truth that will set them free (John 8:31-32).

Like newborn babies, long for the pure milk of the Word . . . .
1 Peter 2:2

Being a Worker at Home: Teach Diligence

How do you feel when you complete a project you have worked on for a long time? How do you feel when you go to bed at night and there is not one dish in the sink and the sink is actually sparkling? It feels good, doesn't it? Help your children feel the delight of completion. Teach them to work with diligence. Today concentrate on diligence with one or more of your children. Don't let your children be lazy.

He who gathers in summer
is a son who acts wisely,
But he who sleeps in harvest
is a son who acts shamefully.
Proverbs 10:5

Being Kind:
With Your Words

Today let every word be kind—every word to your children, to your husband, to your friends, to store clerks and telemarketers, to everyone—and every word about them. Be an example of kindness to your children.

She opens her mouth in wisdom,
And the teaching of kindness
is on her tongue.
Proverbs 31:26

Being Subject to Your Husband: Hold Your Tongue

Some homeschooling mothers are married to godly men who lead their families well, while others are married to non-Christians; but each of us is married to a man who is disobedient to the Word in some areas. Our husbands are married to women who are disobedient, too. We are all sinners in need of God's grace. We need to be submissive so our husbands may be won by the behavior of their wives—without a word. Today be chaste and respectful. Help your husband overcome his sins by seeing your godliness—not by hearing your rebuke. Today hold your tongue.

*. . . be submissive to your own husbands
so that even if any of them are disobedient
to the word, they may be won without a word
by the behavior of their wives, as they
observe your chaste and respectful behavior.*
1 Peter 3:1–2

Loving Your Husband: Be a Suitable Helper

God created each of our husbands to be unique. Think about your husband. What are his specific needs and desires? How could he use your help today? Think about how you can be his suitable helper. Do something today to help him with a specific need.

Then the Lord God said,
"It is not good for the man
to be alone;
I will make him a helper
suitable for him."
Genesis 2:18

Loving Your Children: Know Them

God created each of your children to be unique. He has knit them together and He knows every detail about each of them. Get to know each of your children individually, so you can help them become the people God wants them to be.

Train up a child in the way he should go,
Even when he is old he will not depart from it.
Proverbs 22:6

Loving Your Children: Share Your Faith with Them

Talk to your children about your own faith. Tell them about ways God has answered your prayers. Tell them what you are learning from the ways God is disciplining you. Read your children a verse that has been a special comfort to you. Share your faith with your children today.

For I am mindful of the sincere faith within you,
which first dwelt in your grandmother Lois and your mother Eunice,
and I am sure that it is in you as well.
2 Timothy 1:5

Being Sensible: Teach Your Children to Live

You will feel less pressure if you realize that your children are learning all the time. Be disciplined about completing the curriculum you believe God wants your children to learn, but quit hurrying up to "finish your schoolwork" so you can go on vacation (which can be geography and maybe science and history, too) or get to soccer practice (health and PE) or fix dinner (home economics and science and math). Fill your lives with rich experiences, godly people, and service to others. Don't let "school" be a pressure, learn to live instead. Today look for the learning opportunities in the activities of life.

. . . I came that they may have life,
and have it abundantly.
John 10:10

Being Pure: True Distinction

We want our children to live productive lives. We want them to experience joy. We want them to make good use of their talents. Ultimately, though, we want our children to live with God forever. The other goals we have for them pale in comparison. We've heard of homeschoolers who win the National Spelling Bee and those who get full scholarships to Ivy League universities. God gives some of His children honor and titles of distinction, but let us be content if our children are simply walking in purity.

It is by his deeds that a lad distinguishes himself
If his conduct is pure and right.
Proverbs 20:11

Being a Worker at Home: Make Your Home Guest-Friendly

Jesus spent time in Bethany at the home of two sisters, Mary and Martha, and their brother, Lazarus. What do you think made Him want to be there? Think of ways to make your home a place where others want to be. Be comfortable in your home. Whether simple or grand, your home can be a place that welcomes guests. What will make you feel comfortable about having people visit your home? Do you need to give it a good cleaning? Do you need to tidy up your school things? Do something to make your home—and your heart—more welcoming to guests. A welcoming home can give hope to people who have never known such a home of their own.

. . . I was a stranger, and you invited Me in.
Matthew 25:35

Being Kind: Teach Your Children to Love Each Other

Many accept sibling rivalry as natural and unavoidable, but that is not what the Bible teaches. It tells us about the pain and suffering sibling rivalry causes. Remember Joseph and his brothers? Jacob and Esau? The prodigal son and his brother? Don't tolerate sibling rivalry. Don't allow fighting and bickering and making fun of each other. Don't let a child get by with saying, "I was just teasing." What better place do they have to learn to get along, to be kind, and to be tolerant than at home with your family? Teach your children to love each other.

A new commandment I give to you, that you love one another,
even as I have loved you, that you also love one another.
By this all men will know that you are My disciples,
if you have love for one another.
John 13:34–35

Being Subject to Your Husband: As to the Lord

Being subject to another involves trust. Who told us to be subject to our husbands? God did. Do we trust Him? Isn't it wonderful to know that God has put us in subjection? We don't have the responsibility of leadership that our husbands do. Today be thankful that God is trustworthy and that He has given you your husband whom you can trust. Let's also recognize the responsibility our husbands carry and tell them how much we appreciate them for what they do.

Wives, be subject to your own husbands, as to the Lord.
Ephesians 5:22

Loving Your Husband: Be Gentle

Today be gentle with your husband. Smile gently. Give him a gentle pat every chance you get. Give him gentle hugs and kisses. Speak gently. Enjoy the assurance that this is precious in the sight of God.

[Let your adornment be]
the hidden person of the heart,
with the imperishable quality
of a gentle and quiet spirit,
which is precious in the sight of God.
1 Peter 3:4

Loving Your Children: Forget the World's Mold

Many people—the world, the church, your family, your friends—are telling you how to rear your children. They ask you questions that make you think you don't quite measure up. They ask your children questions about things you haven't taught them yet and then you fear you aren't doing a good enough job. Let God tell you how to rear your children, what they need to know, what they need to do at age 8 and at age 18. Today seek what God says in His Word and refuse to listen to those nagging doubts that people have placed in your heart.

And do not be conformed to this world,
but be transformed by the renewing of your mind,
so that you may prove what the will of God is,
that which is good and acceptable and perfect.
Romans 12:2

Being Sensible:
Teach the Way Life Really Is

Schools divide learning into subjects, like English, math, and science. Adults' lives are not divided into neat little categories; why should children's lives be structured that way? Perhaps spending our childhood and young adulthood in traditional schools where life was divided into categories made it hard for us to adjust to the "real world" of interruptions. I believe children learn better when they see how things are connected. If you have six children doing six subjects each, you are trying to teach 36 subjects! Be sensible. Can you really do that? Give yourself a break. Teach the way life really is.

And he answered, "You shall love the Lord your God
with all your heart, and with all your soul,
and with all your strength, and with all your mind;
and your neighbor as yourself."
And He said to him, "You have answered correctly;
do this, and you will live."
Luke 10:27–28

Being Pure:
Protect Your Children from Evil Companions

Sometimes we worry about whether our children get to spend enough time with children their own age. Do you reject a new friend because she wasn't born the same year you were? Perhaps if God thought it was important that we spend lots of time with people our own ages, we would give birth to litters! Instead, He usually gives us one child at a time, and our new baby comes into a family that has people of varying ages. Guard your children's friendships. Don't assume that because a child is the same age as your child, is homeschooled, or goes to your church, that he or she is automatically a good companion for your child. Protect your children from evil companions.

I am a companion of all those who fear You,
And of those who keep Your precepts.
Psalm 119:63

Being a Worker at Home: Sit at Jesus' Feet

One day Martha welcomed Jesus into her home. She was busy, working hard at her preparations. Meanwhile, her sister Mary sat at the feet of Jesus listening to His Word. Sometimes the best work we can do at home is to sit at Jesus' feet and listen to His Word. When we do that, we get strength to do our work at home and our children learn where to get their strength, too.

But the Lord answered and said to her, "Martha, Martha,
you are worried and bothered about so many things;
but only one thing is necessary, for Mary has chosen the good part,
which shall not be taken away from her."
Luke 10:41–42

Being Kind:
Teach Your Children to Forgive

God cares about how we treat each other. He knows that we are going to disappoint one another. Since He has thought of everything we need, He has even provided a way for us to handle those disappointments. He has not only given us His forgiveness for our sins, but has also taught us and given us the capacity to forgive one another. Forgiveness is one of the kindest things we can do for one another. Teach your children to settle their differences with others and truly forgive from the heart. It is one of the best gifts you will ever give them.

Be kind to one another,
tender-hearted, forgiving each other,
just as God in Christ also has forgiven you.
Ephesians 4:32

Being Subject to Your Husband: Rise Above Fear

"Sarah obeyed Abraham, calling him lord, and you have become her children if you do what is right without being frightened by any fear." That is what God tells us in 1 Peter 3:6. How much of what we do in homeschooling is controlled by fear? Let's obey our husbands and not be frightened by any fear. Let's fear God and not let worldly fears dictate what we do or how we feel.

There is no fear in love;
but perfect love casts out fear,
because fear involves punishment,
and the one who fears
is not perfected in love.
1 John 4:18